Resin

Resin

POEMS

Geri Doran

LOUISIANA STATE
UNIVERSITY PRESS
BATON ✤ ROUGE

First printing

DESIGNER: AMANDA MCDONALD SCALLAN
TYPEFACE: MINION
PRINTER AND BINDER: THOMSON-SHORE, INC.

Library of Congress Cataloging-in-Publication Data
Doran, Geri, 1963–
    Resin : poems / Geri Doran.
        p. cm.
    ISBN 0-8071-3075-3 (cloth ; alk. paper) — ISBN 0-8071-3076-1 (pbk. :
alk. paper)
    I.Title.
PS3604.073R47 2005
811'.6—DC22

                                                        2004024754

The paper in this book meets the guidelines for
permanence and durability of the Committee on
Production Guidelines for Book Longevity of the
Council on Library Resources. ♾

FOR

Howard Doran

AND

Irene Doran

CONTENTS

Resin

We rowed all night in the river of God,
singing *kyrie, kyrie.*

Tonight Is a Night Without Birds

The sky fell open to a map of the constellations.
Earlier the snowmelt reconfigured the field.
I tried to describe it, but the field transformed
into the plains of the soul pressed flat.

Fierceness and moonlight, I thought I'd write,
but the stars outshine the moon and the brightest
star, at any rate, is on the ground and a continent
away. My brightest star is a continent away.

Looking up from the cobbled path in a swath
of darkness darker than any Portland night,
I see a skyful of nightbirds, but none of them's singing.
Like Orion, they're keeping an obstinate silence.

Across the continent, Orion is probably drenched.
Anyway, it is unlikely my love is watching the sky.
A star-flush sky makes the earth seem flat.
Dryness and flatness are the ways a field inhabits a body.

I do not know much about fields, apart
from this amassment of dry grass leaning down.
I know about starry skies. I know silent birds.

Daylilies of Shiloh

Now the eyes of Israel were dim for age,
so that he could not see.
　　　　　—GENESIS 48:10

What fetches up is noise: reeds,
slurp of wavelets bearing wood
sundered from an unlikely ark.

I am moved to prophesy
in a field of hideous bloom.
Pigsty, lilyfield—what difference
to an old man losing sight?
Am smell. Am a thousand reeds humming.
And the hum takes shape.

Favor the good. Favor the right.
Sons shade like the skins of nations,
each darker than the next.
The next to last all shadow now,
who was most light.

Days extend beyond themselves.
I am change. Am a hot excess
favoring the boy like water.

Am daylily nearing sundown, reckless as that.

4

Thin

. . . to my surprise, they only seemed
likenesses if they were long and thin.
—ALBERTO GIACOMETTI

Never in the revealing
did I add weight.
The white line of story
was a horizon line
canted up, a crescendo
of sound tramming
down, *going vertical.*
But into what, exactly?
With what scarab in hand?
My underworld is what
lay east of the horizon,
my heaven what lay west
before the inscrutable tilt.
The symmetry of this story
is a dream of the ocean
plain. Words drift. I'll say
what I mean: A man
I loved was tall and thin,
the skin of him stretched
white over ridges of bone
beside me. Then he stood,
and music rippled down.
Now east is south. Now
here's another Giacometti
nude: chipped away,
pressed in by thumbs.
Love's perfect likeness—
too frail, too brittle,
too thin.

Hurry the Iowa Cornfields

Harder to live a life than cross a field.
—RUSSIAN PROVERB

Twice now in the declining light
I've carried my prayer to the field,
the flashlight's fluttering oval

like lamplight in a library not yet dark—
a shield of the wary
against inescapable consequences.

And though I make my bid
in a field of near-ripe corn,
my floundering god refuses me,

leaves me the rattle of stalks,
the shapes of my desires
numerous and thin.

Here it is nothing to remember
the purblind shriek of the bird,
domestic and white,

sensing hawk—nothing
to remember its idiot call,
here I am, caged.

If caged, you dare not call.
Yet to a field of corn I cannot cross
I come at dusk to stand in the rows,

rummaging in inadequate light
for gold silk turned to brown,
for ripeness, answering.

A Field of Hay

The highway banks over Devil's Slide.

Beyond that nothing is certain. Netting holds
the rocks against the hillside, the hillside

against its weighted base. I imagine
no freehold in this sunstruck place. Only
the road to Pescadero, a left turn

to the redwoods, wide channels of bark
sheltering in the green-slanted shade.

Finally it's shade I desire.
No matter what I said before.

Or in place of the road slinking along the coast,
imagine a fruit stand with a painted sign:
The Farmer's Daughter in red,

a canopied box the size of a horse stall.
I'm not sure yet what to put in this box—

the fruit not in season, and dust kicking up
from the tractor in the field behind.

The barn back home empty a quarter-century,
torn down. The barn with the pitched roof

and the loft we rented to keep the hay in.

Dad driving over slow, the tractor bucket
full, two of us in the loft door picking off

the bales and scooting them inside. Two girls
glad to be at work.

The hay wanted three trips, sometimes
four. The extra bales went in the shack
that was our horse stall now.

Old man Dwyer gone, his trailer hauled away
along with his collection of comic books.

Thirty years collecting them and junk cars
he left in the field behind his place.

Dirty Dwyer.

Living alone in a trailer with a lean-to shack
in a field with no trees for shade.

And those comic books
in knee-high stacks all around the double-wide
that sometimes he'd let me look at.

Before he died and we took to haying.

Retrospective

What carried us from year to year was yield:
potatoes in, potatoes out, like rowing.
Fist-sized, firm, rich tasting and abundant—
of such abundance we could eat them all
winter long and have some left for seed.
It seemed holy even then, to harvest
red and russet, shake the moist earth
from the tuber, feel its heft and lob
it on the pile soon to be transported
to the fruit room (dirt floor and damp cement,
tomatoes on the vine, apples, potatoes).
An earthy flourish of the immanent.

Spring, and quartering the rest to plant,
one eye, at least, per chunk. Father crouched
over the hoe. When did I learn to see
paternal love in seed potatoes planted
with a grunt? Or catechism in the rhythm
beat out as he sowed, tamping down the dirt?

Dusk in the Palm of the Lord

God in the blue-like green dusk.
God in the presence or absence of love.
I forget which grace is. Here I am,
walking to a river with seven bridges
to learn the lesson of crossing over.
I have looked to words for passage.
I have looked to men and found them
wanting water the green-like color of dusk,
my body as bridge. This iron span.
This lattice of iron draws me.
I am one of many choices. I am one grace.
Do not forget me in presence or absence.
Do not forget me at dusk.

Most Heaven, you bring to the door
the unnamable,

holy.

Self-Portrait as Miranda

My story begins at sea, in the bitter liquid.
If not, it would begin in Florida, along I-95
in the circular drive of a circular, lime-green motel.
But I have selected the sea, and you must

trust me on this. Truly terrible stories
begin in navigational error, a slight misreading
of the sight that sets the crew in a maelstrom.
Perhaps in another story it would be a man

standing at the door, surprised that he's knocked,
that you have, in turn, answered. He wishes
now that he had lingered in that drive, paused
before resuming the course toward your door.

As the crew, in desperate but unspoken straits,
wishes belatedly for a drag on the anchor.
Frequently, we are thus carried along.
Frequently, *de profundis,* we struggle ashore

to find ourselves, if not stranded, then beached.
We are inclined to be grateful for land.
Survivors of shipwreck cast two shadows:
the outline of interrupted light, and an aura, thirst

to drown again. Perhaps, in the unwritten story,
the man at the door looks thirsty. You sense
he has come to repair himself at the dry dock
of your flesh. There is nothing else to do.

Your home is an island of white sand
and he wades in from the shoals of the walkway
asking for fresh water. So you find him berth.
This much Miranda herself could explain:

how Ferdinand come shimmering from the sea
appeared no less a rescuer than she,
with his handful of kelp and the pretty words
of a man desperate for sanctuary.

Ferdinand missed that she was shipwrecked
too. Miranda had the shadowy thirst.
You know the rest of the story.
They're happy. Then it ends in the bitter sea.

Blue Moon

Tonight
this hillbilly moon, thick and smug
in a gauze yellow tent-dress,
commands the sky she says
this is my sky don't you forget now
she says *you can call me Blue*
just because she's happened back.
There's a chirr in the pond, the rustle
of water spangles amove with turtle;
over here a crane's ugly stepsister
hectors an interloping hare.
Life's abuzz with drama
and we haven't spoken in months—
the silence as bricky between us
as between Matisse's two girls,
jaundiced and country-song blue
over a plate of desultory eggs.
Let me say exactly what happened:
over sunnysides up you crooned
I won't wrack the end with clichés,
there's nothing can be done
as smug as this comeback moon.
And now she's out, twitching
her hips across this sky saying *Girl*
you have got to let go.
I say *Moon, what happens happens*
once in a blue, backlit June.

Fidelity

after Joseph Brodsky

Fidelity is the movement of the bedroom
into touch: a transposition of rumpled
sheets to the avenues of the fingertips.
Removed from the locus of sex, touch
carries memory, a portmanteau
intimacy: longing, exclusion, union
speakable in the open light of day—
hair brushed back behind an ear,
hands entwined. To hold *another,*
to make casual contact with the nape
of a neck, how insidiously will the hand
begin to possess, demanding the other's
skin be as soft as the lover's, demanding
numerous others, attempting
to satiate what is, finally, insatiable:
the need to have been singular.
The creases in the bedsheets
are a map. The roadways you know
will bring you to uncharted places.

Blue Plums

You entered me like migraine, left
like migraine a private vacancy.
The darkness outside is great and wild.
Blue plums falling from an old tree
demand we believe in wildness,
fallingness. What's the matter is memory,
shrivel and tart. How in this sweet
aftermath of everything the mind
should settle on plums (blue plums!)
is one of the mysteries. That God
and my window-blinds should conspire
to refract the light to look like plums.
Out in the wild nothing.

The body recalls its anniversaries.
Last year, mine loosened and fell.
Now this trembling. This wilderness.
As though I'm waving you a primitive
and dangerous farewell.

City of Bridges

East Portland, 1887

In the distance, colors fade
like broadcloth poorly dyed.

A vagrant sky mirrors the flat gray
of the bridgework; below,

water mirrors the transient sky.
Only the laborers persist, frozen

by the sluicing rain
that slicks the steel girders

and makes them more than heavy,
more unwieldy than seemed possible

only yesterday, when work meant *work*
and *wage* and *shelter*. None of it.

Work is the brute thrust of the steel,
cold oblivion of pelting rain,

mudslips. Work is the cry of the girl
from up on Asylum Street

gone in the river.

The Bridgetown Iron Works Fire

> *There is exchange of all things for fire*
> *and of fire for all things . . .*
> —HERACLITUS OF EPHESUS

Measure the blackened timber,
test its capacity for bearing weight.

Is it sound? Will it make a place,
still, to house the sturdier metal—

an intimate structure of oak,
warm to the touch?

Compare the two under fire:
wood transformed to accordion charcoal,

bitter and dark; while metal,
molten and golden, exchanged nothing,

became nothing more or less.
The phases of wood are a means

of dead reckoning: burn what is built
and gauge your passage

by what is lost.
Let fire have this: the iron works.

Let fire have the onway, the bridge,
leaving us stranded and flushed.

Asylum Street

In architectural renderings,
the asylum is palatial,

governed by formal rules.
Brick bears up well.

Timber, cut from nearby forest
and planed by hand,

sags where the artist dipped
his pen, no doubt tired

from a long day's work.
Or perhaps the wood was green,

improperly cured. Here in the hospital,
cures are often green—

this malady or that
new to the annals of disease.

A clerk maddened from fright by fire,
two sawyers' wives prone to fits

caused by the menses—
these are understood.

But what of the flaxen-haired girl
who thinks she's a sparrow?

She'll make her knocking flight
down polished marble hallways

and take wing above the river
before anyone guesses

that restraint
is mainly an illusion.

Not Unlike the Bridge of Sighs

At confluence, two rivers
form one water, a unified theory

of motion. Small eddies resist,
struggling against the liquid grain,

the water's utilitarian praxis.
There is no need. This theory

incorporates minor incursions,
calls them ebb and flow,

as though the movements were oceanic.
Such water requires a singular bridge—

old, fashioned of wrought iron
with a bascule lift.

Only such a bridge could bear
the commerce of the day:

concourse of the men of industry,
whose silvery glances

meet the visiting physician's.
An Asylum is not a prison

in every sense of the word.
In one sense, it is just

an artist's drawing. In one sense,
a bridge merely draws

the sighs of gilded cagelings,
which are sometimes caught

by the masts of passing ships
and pulled downstream.

White Nile

For pain, forgetting is an island of flowers.
—EDMOND JABÈS

At the equator
rises the father of all rivers.
　Ptolemy envisioned mountain peaks
　　with snow caps,
a glacial progenitor whose steep passage
　spurred a river running north.

Milky white waters
lap three shores. Two are thornbush and shrub.
　The third, superimposed, is a field
　　of sad men
drinking loss. *On this placid bank they forget,*
　Sibyl says to Aeneas,

origin, headstream.
Tutsi crouch in the ebony stands
　along the Kagera, machetes
　　clutched in hand.
Sibyl, can we forget our slaughtered bodies?
　What river here has the balm?

Start south, in the gorge.
In the Sudd's heat, burn off half: water,
　memory. Wander the banks until
　　you are safe—
like Io, from the gadfly; like a hippo
　in the water hyacinth.

Beyond the 45th Parallel

I want alchemy from this ocean,
not these metaphors of endlessness.
I have driven two hundred miles in a rented car
for alchemy. Past the Burnt Woods
and the Chitwood Bridge. Over
the 45th Parallel marked by a small sign.
They are *all* small signs, he'd say—
but he'd mean something literal
about the footlong oblong, the green
behind white lettering. While I
imagine grass limp in the equatorial sun,
snow adrift at the pole—equidistance
compressed to a metal slate.

Like alchemy, endlessness is a fiction.
We are always halfway to somewhere.
I want more than transmutation:
I want the god I pray to to be real.

The wildness had leached out
of the pear trees.

Lord, Yours Is the Hour of Conquest, Mine to Submit

Are You the grease-backed reptile cooling in mud?
                            Dirty One,
all teeth and scurvy intention, what am I that hugs Your back?
(Oh, what am I that's crawling?)
                            I do not know what I do,
forgive me. Gather me beggared like weeds against Your skin.

You are the rupture of slack ponds gone pea green. It matters
nothing. Make me the slit the gator slips between.

Near Grozny, Chechnya

January 1995

Across a field, a woman carries the sack she has slung
    over her shoulder,
a sack that in my country would be burlap, but that in hers
    is something else.
This field the television frames: weedy, with a little snow,
    the woman,
and electrified barbed wire curling around a post.
    Together,
they seem a symbol of destitution, the rough-cut oats in the sack
    a month's provender.
I imagine the woman's pain—a flap on her bootsole folding
    under, exposing
her foot—certain a tear forms in her eye. Regardless,
    I am wrong.
A newsman voices over, that in this place the fighting strayed
    from the city
Russia wants to put down and which the reporter cannot enter
    due to the crossfire.
I see now. The woman is a soldier; the sack of grain a weapon
    riding piggyback.

Barn Burning

The cold surmise that had begun to dawn, drawn as it yet was
    from the uncollected
miasma of notice, watch, drawn even from the croonings
    of midday hunger
 hurrying itself briefly into thought, the porch vacant, then, of thick
    gutteral drawls
while stomachs filled, fortifying themselves for the long hot sun
    of post-meridian
man-talk and watch, and drawn, too, from the unspoken unity
    of men not divided
by commerce or by wives, men whose farms and wives were
    self-sufficing,
or men who had forsaken farms and wives for town, linens and board
    paid by the week;
this vague surmise, working slowly from subconscious into
    whittling-knife
and wood, the rub of chair and porch, the throat-clearing shift
    of galvanizing bodies,
that restless, wordless preamble to speech; this surmise burst
    in telegraphic fragments
unclotted with a cough and coughed back into fearful, outraged
    silence at the admission,
the men bested, not by man or gun, nor by vagaries of heat or rain,
    but by their own surprised voice
(he's passing us, too?) guessing at what the women had known
    for certain, women
who had not divined from languid watching and rocking, who knew,
    separate, percipient,
what the men only eventually surmised (their communal surprise
    embracing their wives,
 too, this female knowledge as sudden to them as the man encroaching,
    though omnipresent
and ancient as his unstoppable gain, his stain of industry propelled
    by pride and shame,
more pride than shame, but shame also, coeval, a singular stalk
    driving from twin roots);

this finally they understood: the man had been passing forever,
    had forever passed
back beyond his father's first lit match to the first match ever lit,
    and farther back
to a god's transgression in passing fire to man, but more than fire—
    no, fire's thieving use.

Rosary

Gloria Patri, black mortal bead,
harbor us, alleviate our fear.
Be a marbled gem to ransom death
from her maternal care.

Lacrimae Rerum

Volgograd, the Bones

Like a tangle of jewels in grandmother's box,
    or twigs worked loose from last season's
robins' nest, like haphazard sprays of driftwood
    lacing sand, the bones of Peschanka repose
in splendid decay, bask in the nimbus of old Stalingrad.
    City of ermine and ice, grand reliquary
of submarine factories, your Wehrmacht soldiers,
    cold- and gun-routed bodies,
lie like embellished privations in grandfather's story.

A thousand white nights you've slept, pretty city,
    while your enemy rocked in their beds.

       ∞

A cordon of buildings as mottled as verde antique
    rises like new Berlin—impassioned, bleak—
the portal is built from a measure of wire;
    it reads Arbeit Macht Frei
in wiry script.
            Schoolgirls chalk their names
    on the street. The one with dark eyes
       erases hers with her feet.

       ∞

What confessionary chapel is as hushed?
    Bones litter the steppes,
dog tags spilled onto spines, here and there
    a makeshift ribcage trellis.
          Small scaffoldings for grief.

St. Peter's Chains

Swam for a moment in the cautious dip
    of neck and shoulder,
chafed on his coarse skin, and shuddered loose
    in negligeed light,
a fold of angel beckoning him. A harvest of mind,
    this thresh and reap
of meaning: he saw a sheetful of beasts
    beatific, redeemed.

    ∞

At Dachau, in the women's latrine, was a vanity
    fashioned thus: a wooden box,
a triangle of mirror culled from the *Oberfuhrer*'s bin.
    She made this, the woman
who cleaned, to see what vestiges of beauty
    remained.
             Tell me.
Who are the common? Who the unclean?

Recitative

Told to love the diminished thing, this world
    whose fall is never quite complete,
which tumbles down these vine-entrusted decades
    to the century's waiting feet;

told we can love this world still, who find
    its random consolations brief
(a creek whose drying fingers vein
    the landscape like a leaf);

told this, O incarnata, word made flesh,
    do we lay this failed world at your crèche?

Cedar of mercy,

I commend into your arms
this moving river.

Resin

The needled air of the lodgepole.
Sting of pine at the base of your throat.
"A cold snap," he says. "Coming on."

Believing wasn't always hard.
The river forked in three: I knew
truth could go in different ways.

Corn was ripe when the tassels turned.
Late. Later still, potatoes to be dug—
how far out, and how deep down,

I knew. Could slant the shovel right.
I'd use my hands now, claw deep
to better cup them, one by one,

as they let go their hold on earth.
This is the soil that I am from.
Those mountains—there, the Swan,

the Mission Range, and west the Salish—
they all washed down to fill this place.
We gained by their diminishment.

The harvest's passed to other hands.
The house is sold. The sap's curling
deep into the pines. "The weather's

turned," he says. I work the pump;
I try to slough the dirt stains off.
"Predictable as an Indian."

The Madronas and the Mystery

The madrona tree I believe in.

Consider its hue of persuasion:
copper pennies under the bark

with the papery coils. Pennies
going red as dusk settles in.

To be precise, going ruby red.
Faith is a grove of madronas

weighing the limits,
hull and leaf. Their shade exact

as the day goes down.

In love with the subterranean—

layers of sediment
that grew up out of bedrock—

time sheeted itself between.
What we know of it

are fragments impressed
with indecipherable script.

Time ravishes us.

The scrawl of it.
And the mystery.

Most of it hidden underground forever.

I began with a train
on the Union Pacific line—

seduction of industry
and locomotion. How it ravished me

on the way to work one day.
Only the rattle of boxcars

became a stand of madrona trees
considering the mystery.

What calculus of logic explains that?

Love, bedrock, trees the color
of rubies.

Answer me that.

Lives of the Gods, Lives of the Saints

for Tom Spanbauer

So little darkness in the darkness here.
Each leaf a mirror of moonlight, incomparable.
The Japanese maple spooncupped in gold

is Medusa in the old tale, her hair astir.
Indoors, the wandering Jew makes its pitch
for the wall, thinking *I am a constant lover,*

twists back, falls short. Are we always
measured by what we do not reach?
What holds us here, out over the emptiness,

is a causeway of cells and light, nothing
more than a dream of crossing.
Somehow a saint or two ever perched, there

on the levered arms of the drawbridge,
bartering safe passage for their human charge.
Outside, the maple moves like lamentation.

Medusa keening in her grief.
Is our call to the gods always outcry?
If they came, like the saints, to listen,

would we ever find ourselves
spooncupped in light?
Would we settle for being held?

Forgiven

The year I began to see trees
in the studied shapes of your leaving
was the year I learned to love botany.

Late December, I walked to your work
gripping the small stub of a lie
and risked, for once, the wild declaiming

of arms that find themselves empty.
Never mind the handful of proof.
Now the move comes naturally,

my arms flying up to take the shape
of any given tree. Madrona arms,
sequoia arms. Is this the form

of *any* feeling? For, given feeling,
there is little left but the trees—
madrona, sequoia, birch,

box elder, and my one beloved
cedar of Lebanon—
that gives shape to me.

The Bitter Season

Letter I

Once, this shadow of mountain peaks
    meant the town itself closed down,
        settled in like farmhouse walls
    onto firm foundations.
Thin puffs of smoke sank into the night,
        brief, nubile ghosts

no one wanted. And why not ghosts
    if flesh itself—translucent,
        bored with neglect—is nothing
    more than transfigured flight?
Nothing but a signaled departure,
        more flare than flame.

    In this light cast
by a mountain-scarred moon,
        nothing settles,
    no change overcomes us:
the town is no town
        reduced to sleep.

In each room, a woman or man
    wakes to the radiant skin
        of a lover, a flesh-ghost
    caught in the act: sleeping,
receding. Or is it just one room,
        one man asleep,

one wife unsettled by a moon,
    who discerns in his shoulder's
        arc her own trajectory,
    her frankest wish to carve
this shape, hold it still and firm and right—
        as dark holds light.

Letter II

Everything depends upon position:
a rocket launched in Florida translates
to a falling star in Poulsbo. At ease on the deck,

a woman may be forgiven for missing it,
her vantage slightly forward, her focus
backward, on the spritz of light

the rocket sheds going up. She bought it,
man on the moon, a universe explained
by planetary nebulae, a small dispersion

of light in the darkness, everything
rising upward and forging ahead.
She hadn't thought about it coming down.

Though here on the deck, the family
muses on the frequency of falling
as though it were an ordinary thing—

this plummet from the heavens.

Letter III

O why did we forfeit the lean grass of Florida
    Why did we walk
unknowing into the punishing rains with no sticks
    just our wrecked knees
I am staring down at a strange roof a garden
    of metal shafts
like oil rigging or a peculiar type of steam vent
    and all I can see
is the roof next door to our two-story building
    cluttered with junk
a bicycle a bedspring and miscellaneous debris
    Wasn't it good
though sometimes lying in bed with the slant light
    streaming in
sometimes at night walking in the rain we thought
    might fortify us
Wasn't it sometimes more of a forked flame
    than a sodden mess
Now there's this tree outside my window—my view
    has changed—and this crooked tree
small with wild spikes and a covering of snow looks
    like a deranged bonsai
and you're not here to share the joke you damn fool
    We were damn fools
to think we could outlast the rain just look who does
    just look at that

Letter IV

Our plumb line found vertical. Gravity's
fantasy. Now I live hardscrabble on this hill.
As if on the sheer, with pebbles rolling down.
Where it is level, I am offered large stones
that resemble sarcophagi. Each sheltered
by a small bush. This is no religious rite.
I am neither the passionate blue blaze
nor the equanimity of funereal rock.
Lately, I remember a man in Gainesville
who ran all day with his arms in the air.
Shouting praise or muttering prayers.
O running man in Florida, I understand.
See, my arms also are in the air.

Reveal, in the Country Moonlight, Your Steadfast Means

My body is a field of dark-held white. Trace on me
    the map of Your will.

The Cedar of Lebanon

We rowed all night in the river of God,
singing *kyrie, kyrie.*

Mercy.

That is the part I never understand.
The garden wall sooty and short.
Snapdragons queer and abundant,

then the dry land rivering up
for all the world like the Venice canals:

dark and holy. And only us watching.
Watching, there in the yard,

the soul of the earth become the soul
of the water, moving.

The two of us singing *kyrie,*
and afterwards parting it as we passed

from knowing into unknowing and back.

∞

What does it mean, *ward off,*
keep from?

Most Heaven, you bring to the door
the unnamably homely.

Desire, like a kitchen wife.
The floor, her floor. The knife,

her knife.

∞

Again.
What does it mean ward off?

He says, this protects you,
this mask at the gate.

∽

What I meant when I said the wildness
had leached out of me

the way it leached out of the pear trees
in their old, old rows in the orchard

up at Powell Butte
was that water can wick you dry.

∽

Cedrus libani, tree of Asia,
cedar of mercy,

I commend into your arms
this moving river.

(Grant me nothing. Or grant
me this.)

ACKNOWLEDGMENTS

Poems from this volume, or versions of them, first appeared in the following publications. Many thanks to the editors for their encouragement.

American Poet: "The Bitter Season" (Letter IV), "The Cedar of Lebanon" (fourth section), and "Thin." *The Atlantic Monthly:* "Resin" and "Retrospective." *New England Review:* "Barn Burning," "Beyond the 45th Parallel," "Blue Moon," "Blue Plums," "City of Bridges," "Daylilies of Shiloh," "Dusk in the Palm of the Lord," "Hurry the Iowa Cornfields," "Tonight Is a Night Without Birds," and "White Nile." *The New Republic:* "Lord, Yours Is the Hour of Conquest, Mine to Submit" and "The Cedar of Lebanon" (first section). *TriQuarterly:* "Self-Portrait as Miranda." *The Virginia Quarterly Review:* "Lives of the Gods, Lives of the Saints."

To Carolyn Altman, William Logan, David Roderick, and C. Dale Young for gracious help with this book, much gratitude. The Wallace Stegner Program at Stanford offered a matchless blend of financial support, community, and encouragement; I will always appreciate my time there. Literary Arts, the Millay Colony for the Arts, and the Sewanee Writers' Conference also provided much-needed support and hospitality.

To Henri Cole for selecting the book, my enduring thanks.

In the words of Robert Lowell, I make these *admissions and disclosures.* I am indebted to "Stalingrad: Letters from the Dead" by Timothy Ryback (*The New Yorker,* February 1, 1993) for several facts in the poem "Lacrimae Rerum." In the poem's final section, phrases are borrowed from Robert Frost and Hart Crane. "Barn Burning" retells part of William Faulkner's Snopes trilogy, echoing passages of *The Hamlet.* Part four of "City of Bridges" quotes "The Report of the Inspecting Physician of the Insane Asylum of Oregon" (September 1872). Poems by Lucie Brock-Broido and Joseph Brodsky were suggestive of syntax or theme in, respectively, "Daylilies of Shiloh" and "Fidelity." There may be other borrowings, now lost; I offer my grateful if incomplete acknowledgment.